What Animal Has These Parts?

NOSE

AMY CULLIFORD

A Crabtree Roots Book

CRABTREE
Publishing Company
www.crabtreebooks.com

School-to-Home Support for Caregivers and Teachers

This book helps children grow by letting them practice reading. Here are a few guiding questions to help the reader with building his or her comprehension skills. Possible answers appear here in red.

Before Reading:
- What do I think this book is about?
  - *I think this book is about noses.*
  - *I think this book is about animals that have noses.*
- What do I want to learn about this topic?
  - *I want to learn what different noses look like.*
  - *I want to learn which animal has the longest nose in the world.*

During Reading:
- I wonder why...
  - *I wonder why elephants have really long noses.*
  - *I wonder why some animals have colorful noses.*
- What have I learned so far?
  - *I have learned that noses can be big or small.*
  - *I have learned that animal noses can be different colors.*

After Reading:
- What details did I learn about this topic?
  - *I have learned that noses can be different shapes and sizes.*
  - *I have learned that most animals have noses.*
- Read the book again and look for the vocabulary words.
  - *I see the word **elephant** on page 5 and the word **monkey** on page 12. The other vocabulary words are found on page 14.*

What **animal** has a long **nose** like this?

An **elephant**!

Which animals have
little noses like these?

Mice!

Which animal has this red nose?

A **monkey!**

Word List
Sight Words

a	little	this
an	long	what
has	red	which
like	these	

Words to Know

animal

elephant

mice

monkey

nose

26 Words

What **animal** has a long **nose** like this?

An **elephant**!

Which animals have little noses like these?

Mice!

Which animal has this red nose?

A **monkey**!

CRABTREE
Publishing Company

Written by: Amy Culliford
Designed by: Bobbie Houser
Series Development: James Earley
Proofreader: Janine Deschenes
Educational Consultant: Marie Lemke M.Ed.
Photographs:
Shutterstock: Manon van Althuis: cover; Bilanol: p.
1; matthieu Gallet: p. 3, 14; AndreAnita: p. 4, 14;
polya_olya: p. 7; SERGEI BRIK: p. 8-9, 14; Baehaki
Hariri: p. 11, 14; Charlotte Bleijenberg: p. 13-14

What Animal Has These Parts?
NOSE

Library and Archives Canada Cataloguing in Publication

CIP available at Library and Archives Canada

Library of Congress Cataloging-in-Publication Data

CIP available at Library of Congress

Crabtree Publishing Company

www.crabtreebooks.com   1-800-387-7650

Published in the United States
Crabtree Publishing
347 Fifth Avenue, Suite 1402-145
New York, NY, 10016

Published in Canada
Crabtree Publishing
616 Welland Ave.
St. Catharines, ON, L2M 5V6